ISBN 978-1-334-67271-2
PIBN 10757084

This book is a reproduction of an important historical work. Forgotten Books uses state-of-the-art technology to digitally reconstruct the work, preserving the original format whilst repairing imperfections present in the aged copy. In rare cases, an imperfection in the original, such as a blemish or missing page, may be replicated in our edition. We do, however, repair the vast majority of imperfections successfully; any imperfections that remain are intentionally left to preserve the state of such historical works.

NOTES ON THE HISTORY OF THE JEWS IN BARBADOS.

By N. Darnell Davis, C. M. G.

9-27 66 '

NOTES ON THE HISTORY OF THE JEWS IN BARBADOS.

BY N. DARNELL DAVIS, C. M. G.

I.

Extracted by N. Darnell Davis, C. M. G., from Vol. I, Miscellaneous, pp. 397-416, of Manuscript Collections compiled by Dr. Lucas (grandfather of Rev. Charles Kingsley) and now in the possession of E. T. Racker, Esq., of Merview, Hastings, Barbados, West Indies.

These people appeared here very early after the settlement of the country, both Dutch, French, and Portuguese (*sic*) : the French probably from Martinique, for the purposes of smuggling ; the Dutch, I presume, from Holland, when our trade in a manner centered there, and I have always understood that the bulk of them were of Portuguese origin ; which is the highest order among them ; and who in London, neither unite in the same synagogue or burial grounds ; here, however, they must coalesce, from paucity of numbers.

The Portuguese Jews came to us, either directly from the Brazils, or through Surinam when possessed by us, or on its final evacuation by us to the Dutch, 1667.

Soon after the discovery of the Brazils, great numbers of Jews were banished thither from Portugal in 1548. The Dutch invaded the Brazils in 1630 ; and, by 1635 they had conquered nearly the whole country ; and to this source, in the absence of any direct, I attribute the swarms of Jews, formerly found in the West Indies ; for men of their habits were not likely to remain on the theater of war, when they could escape ; and dealing always more in personal than real estate (having no kingdom of their own in which to purchase lands)

11   129

they could more conveniently emigrate. Barbados and Martinique had become places of considerable commerce; Surinam was fast settling, and to those places they removed themselves (Appendix A.). To this source undoubtedly is chiefly owing the early and long-continued circulation of the Portuguese gold coins in this Island; and both the Brazils and the settlements on the east coast of Africa supplied immense sums to Portugal.

This coin came to us as a bullion trade, from London and Portugal, where all the light pieces were bought by weight, and delivered by tare; and we likewise got some false coin.

The Spanish coins were chiefly silver, the returns for Africans sold to the Spaniards by the Royal Company or individuals.

And the reason we had no English money must have been the severe restrictive laws against exporting the coin of the realm, even to her own colonies; and the balance of trade being in her own favor, there was little necessity to make it up by coins.

I find the following notices of them in our early history; and by the very first notices, on the 12th of August, 1656, it will be ascertained that they were here in considerable numbers, and required regulation:

As to the particulars relating to ye Jews presented by the Grand Jury, at the last general Sessions held for this Island, the Governor and Council will take ye same into further consideration at next sitting. (" Minutes of Council," August 12, 1656, p. 248. See Appendix B.)

Upon the Petition presented to ye Governor and Council concerning the Jews, by the Grand Inquest, that ye Laws and Statutes of ye Commonwealth of England relating to Foreigners and Strangers be exactly taken notice of, and put in due execution, by those whom it should or may concern. (" Minutes of Council," August 12, 1656, p. 250.)

Upon ye Petition of Jacob Nunez, Jew, it is ordered that the Judge of ye Court shall see the same; and forthwith cause his Marshal to levy the Execution therein mentioned, according to Law. (" Minutes of Council," August 12, 1656, p. 250.)

The following order of the King in council will best explain itself ("Minutes of Council," August 10, 1681, p. 401):

At the Court of Whitehall, 29th of October 1669
Present:
The King's Most Excellent Majesty.
His Royal Highness ye Duke of Yorke
His Highness Prince Rupert
Lord Archbishop of Canterbury

Earl of Carlisle	Lord Treasurer
Earl of Craven	Duke of Buckingham
Lord Arlington	Duke of Albermarle
Lord Newport	Duke of Ormond
Lord Holles	Earl of Ossory
Lord Treasurer	Earl of Bridgwater
Mr. Vice Chamberlain	Earl of Sandwich
Mr Secretary Trevor	Earl of Bath

Whereas upon the humble Petition of Antonio Rodrigo Rigio, Abraham Levi Regio, Lewis Dias, Isaac Jeraio Coutinho, Abraham Pereira, David Baruch Louzado, and other Hebrews, made free Denizens by His Majesty's Letters Patents, and residing at Barbados (read at ye Board ye 15th of September, 1669), together with a certificate thereunto annexed, complaining, that notwithstanding their Denization, divers persons of said Island do endeavour to deprive them of the benefit thereof, and refuse to admit their testimony in Courts of Judicatures, and expose them to all sorts of injuries in their Trade, and praying relief therein, His Majesty was then graciously pleased in Council to refer the consideration thereof to ye Right Honble, the Lord Willoughby of Parham, His Majesty's Governor of ye Carribee Islands; who was required to report his opinion thereupon, to His Majesty in Council, who delivered in his Report in writing as followeth (vizt):—

"May it please Your Majesty:

"In obedience to Your Majesty in Council's order of ye 15th of September last past, made upon ye Petition of Antonio Rodrigo Rizio, Abraham Levi Rizio, and other Hebrews made free Denizens by Your Majesty's Letters Patents, and residing at Barbados, I have called to my assistance some of the chief Planters, and have considered of the said Petition, and certificate thereunto annexed, and do thereupon humbly Report to Your Majesty, that I do find that Your Majesty's Hebrew subjects in the Island of

Barbados have not been exposed to any other injuries in their Trade, or otherwise, than only such as they conceive redound to them by reason of the non-admittance of their Testimony in Courts of Judicature; whereof also, during my residence on my Government I never received any complaints from them. But I do find it to be true, that the Judges in the Courts of Judicature in Barbados have ever since Your Majesty's most happy Restoration, refused to admit of the Testimony of the Hebrews in such cases wherein Your Majesty's Christian subjects are parties; for that they are of opinion that by ye Law they neither can, nor ought to admit them, since they refuse to swear upon the Holy Gospel, which ye Law requires to be done in ye administration of all oaths, in civil causes depending between Your Majesty's subjects. Nevertheless their Testimony hath been, and is admitted in those courts in all cases depending between Hebrew and Hebrew, to which Your Majesty's Christian subjects are not parties; but I do find, that in the time of the late Usurpation, their Testimonies were then admitted in all Courts, and in all cases whatsoever; and if it shall appear to Your Majesty, that by reason of the present non-admittance of their Testimonies in all cases, they do receive Injury in their Trade (the freedom whereof I do think to be the Interest of that Your Island), I humbly conceive, that if Your Majesty shall be pleased to direct Your Governor to require his Council, and the Assembly there, to prepare and pass an Act or By-Law, for the free admission of their Testimony, as is desired, it will be effectual to that purpose; which I most humbly submit to Your Majesty's Most Princely Wisdom.

" Wm. Willoughby."

Which being this day read at the Board, it was upon due consideration of the whole matter, thought fitt, and accordingly ordered by His Majesty in Council, that ye Right Honble the Lord Willoughby of Parham, the present Governor of the Carribee Islands, and the Governor there for the time being be, and he is hereby directed and authorized to require his Council, and the Assembly there, to pass an Act or By-Law, whereby such Hebrews as shall from time to time be Naturalized by His Majesty, and resident in the said Island of Barbados, shall and may be freely admitted to give their Testimony in the Courts of Judicature there, in such manner and form, as the Religion of the said Hebrews will permit; and such as the Governor for the time being, His Council and the Assembly there, shall allow of; and likewise to enjoy the full benefit of their Naturalization, according to the tenor and purport of His Majesty's Letters Patents.

Richard Browne.

In pursuance of the foregoing royal order the following law No. 61 (M. L.) was passed February 18, 1674, restraining the testimony of the Jews to matters relating to trade and dealing only; and so continued to the year 1786, when it was repealed by No. 40 (M. L.) ; the legislature refusing to grant more though enjoined thereto by the foregoing royal order.

No. 61.   An Act appointing how the Testimony of People of the Hebrew Nation, shall be admitted in all courts and causes.

Whereas His Sacred Majesty hath signified his Royal pleasure, that all persons of the Hebrew Nation resident in this Island, that are made her Denizens may be admitted to give their Testimonies on their oaths, in all Courts and Causes, in such manner and form as the Religion of the said Hebrews will admit.   Be it therefore Enacted and ordained by His Excellency Sir Jonathan Atkins, K^t, Captain General and Chief Governor of this, and other the Carribee Islands, the Council and Assembly of this Island, that all such persons of the Hebrew Nation as reside in this Island, and are men of Credit and Commerce, shall from henceforth be freely admitted before all Judges, Justices and other Officers, in all Courts and Causes whatever, relating to Trade and Dealing, and not otherwise, to give their Testimony upon their Oaths, on the five Books of Moses, in such manner and form as is usual, and the Religion of the said Nation doth admit.

Assénted to the 19th of February 1674

Edwin Stede, Dep^{ty} Govr.

The Jews finding their persons not protected by the foregoing enactment, presented the following petition to Sir Richard Dutton, knight, the Governor of that time:

Barbados—   To His Excellency Sir Richard Dutton, Knight, Captain General and chief Governor of Barbados, &c, the Honble Council and Worthy Gentlemen of the Assembly.

The Humble Petition of Aaron Baruch Louzado, Daniel Bueino,[1]

---

[1] Surely Daniel Bueino must be a Portuguese Jew; and perhaps the origin of the present name Bynoe; a name I never met with anywhere else.

and Jacob Formzabe, in the behalf of themselves and the rest of the Jews in this Island humbly sheweth:

That whereas by an Act made and passed by His Excellency Sir Jonathan Atkins, Knight, late Governor of this Island, the Honble Members of the Council and Gentlemen of the Assembly, bearing date of the 18th of February, 1674, it was thereby enacted and ordained, that all such persons of the Hebrew Nation as reside in this Island, and are men of Credit and Commerce, should be admitted before all Judges, Justices and other officers, in all Courts and Causes whatsoever, relating to Trade and Dealing, and not otherwise, to give their Testimony on their Oaths, on the five Books of Moses, in such manner and form as usual, and the Religion of the said Nation doth admit; and whereas also, by an order made and passed by His Excellency Sir Jonathan Atkins, Knight, Governor of this Island, &c, and the Honble Members of the Council, bearing date the 25th of November, 1675,[2] being for the better Confirmation of Peace (the Jews having formerly been threatened by some Christians, by reason whereof they went in fear of their lives), and that they might have the benefit of protection against outrages, by his Majesty's Laws in such case provided, they conforming themselves to the direction of the Laws:

And whereas the said Act and Order, by the Departure of the said Governor, are now become of no force or validity to your Petitioners, whereby they may receive any benefit thereof for recovering of their just debts, and enabling them to trade, traffic, etc., and have commerce with the Christians and to defend themselves against accruing wrongs and injuries, without Your Excellency's tender and prudent consideration of the great hardships and confinement Strangers and Foreigners lie under in such cases, will be graciously pleased to give relief.

Whereof in all humility Your Petitioners implore Your Excellency, the Honble members of the Council, and worthy Gentlemen of the Assembly, to extend your favour so far, as to take the Said Act and Order of Council under your serious and prudent consideration, that the said Act and Order may

---

[2] The order of the 25th of November, 1675, by Sir Jonathan Atkins is wanting—the volume containing it not being in existence, to my knowledge; but the substance of it is in this petition. But see article by Dr. Friedenwald containing it in *Publications of the American Jewish Historical Society*, No. 5, p. 96.

be Revived; or that a new Act or Order of Council may pass to the same intents and purposes, whereby Your Petitioners may not be utterly debarred and disenabled to Trade and Traffic, for acquiring an honest livelihood for their mainte- nance and support in this World.

Barbados.

By His Excellency.

This Petition is referred and recommended to the Assembly to prepare a Bill to enable His Majesty's subjects of the Hebrew Nation resident in this Island, to be admitted to give their Testi- monies in the several Courts of Judicature in this Island, in such manner as the Religion of the Jews will permit, pursuant to His Majesty's Order-in-Council in their behalf made; whereby His Majesty is pleased to command the Governor of this Island for the time being, to require the Council and Assembly to pass an Act or Law for that purpose.

This Board, upon the Petition of the Jews this day presented, having taken into their consideration a former Order here made, in the time of Sir Jonathan Atkins, then Governor, dated the 25th of November 1675, whereby the then Governor and Council for the better preserving His Majesty's Hebrew Subjects residing in this Island, from being beaten, maimed or wounded, did order, that in such cases, the Jews should be permitted to give their own Oath in Evidence, for Proof, before such Justice of the Peace, before whom such complaint should be made; I do declare the said Order to be good and valid, notwithstanding Sir Jonathan Atkins, the then Governor, is not now Governor: and all Judges, Justices of the Peace, and all others are hereby desired to take notice thereof, and give obedience thereto accordingly.

The Jews seem to have been objects of great anxiety with the Barbadians, although they did not aspire to any ascendancy in Church or State, the objects of terror to Episcopalians; and they (the Barbadians) refused to obey not only Sir Jonathan Atkins's order, but even the royal order itself, and would not give them their testimony in all cases, as required; but even passed an act in direct opposition, and kept in their law books for 112 years, viz., to the year 1786, as will be presently seen. And it was not judged expedient by the Lords of Trade, etc., to have it repealed. But even with personal inabilities they exceedingly flourished, till commerce took a new direction; and every difficulty in their dealings with the Christians vanished by their keeping a Christian clerk in their shops to prove their debts and contracts with them.

At length in the year 1786 their testimony was restored to them without a struggle, I believe, by repealing No. 61 (M. L.) by No. 40 (M. L.), as will be seen below, viz.:

Whereas by an Act passed by the Assembly and Council of this Island, and assented to on the 18th day of February 1674, by His Excellency Sir Jonathan Atkins, Knight, then Governor, entitled " An Act appointing how the Testimony of the people of the Hebrew Nation shall be admitted in all Courts and Causes," reciting that his sacred Majesty had signified his Royal Pleasure, that all persons of the Hebrew Nation residing in this Island, that were made free Denizens, might be admitted to give their Testimony on their Oaths, in all Courts and Causes, in such manner and form as the Religion of the said Hebrew Nation would admit; it was therefore enacted, that all such persons of the Hebrew Nation as resided in this Island, and were men of Credit and Commerce, should from henceforth be freely admitted before all Judges, Justices and other officers, in all Courts and Causes whatsoever, relating to Trade and Dealing, and not otherwise, to give their Testimony upon their oaths on the Five Books of Moses, in such manner and form as was usual, and the Religion of the said Nation would admit: and whereas the Said Act having been made expressly Contrary to His then Majesty's Royal Pleasure, by confining the Testimony of persons of the Hebrew Nation to men of Commerce only, and to Causes relating to Trade and Dealing, and not otherwise, which His said Majesty, as by the Preamble of the said Act appears, intended and directed should be general, and extend to all free denizens of that nation in all Courts and in all Causes whatever, the same never received the Royal Confirmation; and not being considered as of force, was omitted by Rawlins, Zouch and Salmon, in their several compilements of the Law of this Island, and never printed, though their respective editions went through different impressions; but remained in the Secretary's Office unnoticed and disregarded, until the year 1762 when an Act having passed authorising Richard Hall, since deceased, to print a new edition of the Laws of Barbados, and the said Richard Hall not finding any actual repeal of the said Act, and conceiving it therefore, from the fact of the record, to be in force, he accordingly had the same printed and published in his said Edition of Laws, as an Act in force, taking notice, however, in a note at the foot of the said Act, that it had never been printed, or even the Title inserted in any former edition; and observing also in his preface, that some of the Acts printed in his collection were not in general use, but that he thought himself not authorised to omit any but those actually and expressly repealed: and whereas the Hebrew Nation, by the Laws and Constitution of England, whether natural-born subjects or aliens are admissable in all Courts and in all Causes whatsoever, both Criminal and Civil, as Witnesses competent to give Testimony, upon their being sworn. upon the Pentateuch; and such has been the constant practice as well in this Island as in England:—for as much therefore as the rejecting of the Testimony of Jews may be subversive of Justice, and attended with infinite inconveniences; Be it Enacted and declared by His Excellency David Parry, Esquire, His Majesty's Captain General Governor, and Commander-in-Chief, etc., etc., etc., that the said recited Act ought not to be in force, but the same and every part thereof is, as is hereby declared to be null and void and absolutely repealed to all intents and purposes.

Passed September 9th, 1786.

This was one among the many acts that had long encumbered and disgraced our code; and No. 82, the very next I shall quote, stands in the same unhappy light, viz., No. 82, in which is this clause against the Jews, repealed however soon after by No. 108, clause 1st.

No. 82. Clause 17. And in regard the Planters' necessity doth compel them for the management only of their Lands, to keep so vast a stock of Negroes and other Slaves, whose desperate lives and great numbers become dangerous to them, and all other the inhabitants; that therefore such who are not bound up by that necessity, in having Plantations of their own, or hired land, may not increase the danger to this Island, by keeping Negroes or other Slaves to hire out to others: Be it therefore enacted by the Authority aforesaid, that no person of the Hebrew Nation, residing in any Sea-port town of this Island, shall keep or employ any Negro or other Slave, be he man or boy, for any use or service whatsoever, more than one Negro or other Slave, man or boy, to be allowed to each of the persons of the said Nation, excepting such as are denizened by His Majesty's Letters Patent, and not otherwise, who are to keep no more than for their own use, as shall be approved of by the Lieutenant Governor, Council and Assembly: and if any Negro, man or boy, more than is before allowed by this Act, shall be found three months after the publication hereof, in the Custody, possession, or use of any of the persons aforesaid, then every such person or persons shall forfeit such Negro or other Slave; one moiety of the value thereof to whomsoever shall inform, and the other moiety to His Majesty to the use in this Act appointed.

They were early dealers in false coin, as well as importers of light coin, as before observed; and their knowledge of the Portuguese language, and its near relative the Spanish, gave them great facilities in dealing with those two nations of bullion. I find the following early order to prosecute one of them recorded April 27, 1682 ("Minutes of Council," p. 459):

Information being given to this Board of Mr. Raphaell de Mercado importing and vending extraordinary light Spanish, which may in time prove a thing of evil consequence by means thereof; and for that it appeared to this Board the information had matter of truth in it; It is therefore ordered, that the said Raphaell de Mercado stand forthwith bound to the Grand Sessions, there to answer the same, himself in £500 sterling; and two sureties in £250, sterling, each: and

that Jeremiah Cooke, Esquires, two of His Majesty's Justices of the Peace, summon the said Mercado before them and take his Recognizance; and likewise that they summon Captain Samuel W. Wiltshire to appear before them, and enter into Recognizance with what other persons whatsoever, to give in evidence against the said Mercado in this matter.

It had been well for us had this prudent foresight of our ancestors not been forgotten in latter times. The practice of importing light Portuguese coins, in particular, extended to a most alarming depreciation of our currency. The papers on light coins and exchanges in the Carribean throw considerable light on the subject; but the unlawful gains of a very few grains in a light moidore or joe, lost by attrition were not even the shadow of a shadow of what we have since seen practiced on the most extensive scale. Moidores that should be worth six dollars were clipped, filed, etc., to the intrinsic value of four; joes of eight dollars to six; and all coins, except those current in Great Britain, in the same proportion.

When the original coins were not to be procured readily in sufficient abundance, for the file and scissors, joes were coined in England, both with ancient and modern dies, very fair to the eye, excellently milled, exactly of the size of the cut-joe, worth six dollars. They were imported in the greatest abundance, and remitted back immediately in bills or produce, at an enormous profit. Others were of the full size of a joe, very thin, with a shrill ring; not that of gold, supposed to be chiefly platina. These were from North America.

The cut-joes, etc., clipped and filed in the country, were not milled. They would not take the trouble to do it.

The evil was of gigantic magnitude, and we were tired with half-measures of honesty; propounded, no doubt, by interested individuals: and when did half-measures ever do any good? At length the legislature appearing incapable or unwilling to do the only possible right thing, viz., giving the coins a currency by weight, fineness and intrinsic value, Governor Parry interposed. He issued three proclamations with the advice of the council: the first two for regulating the silver coins, the third for those of gold. In those for silver, he was constitutionally correct; but not so in that for the gold, which was neither founded on the revival of an old law, nor followed by one legalizing the act, and indemnifying for it. But the good sense of the people prevailed. The measure was so just, and so imperiously called for, that no opposition whatsoever was given to carrying it into immediate execution. The proclamations for the silver were grounded on the 6th Anne, Chap. 30; by which silver was virtually made the only legal tender here, by weight; and which, by the 19th Royal Instruction, he was bound to see carried into execution; but which payment having been much more inconvenient than tale, had been discontinued as much as possible. To the proclamation he annexed, at length, the act; and the measure was effectual. ("Minutes of Council," March 16, 1791, pp. 205 and 211, and instruction at length.)

This act of Anne was a good act when it passed; for much of the Spanish coin of that day was hammered silver and gold, at least dollars and pistoles, called cob-money.[3]

[3] Cob-money, or hammered money, was this: a piece of the metal of the exact fineness and weight of the coin, rounded in shape as much as possible in so rude a production, was hammered on one side with the head of the reigning monarch, and on the other with his arms; very imperfectly done, however. It was thick in the middle, thin in the edges—a rude lump. The word Cob, I understand, in Spanish means a piece or lump of anything. The last Cob-Dollars that I have seen were brought by my Lord Combermere from St. Kitts. They were unknown there; but on showing them to me, and asking information, I explained them to him as old acquaintances. In a late tremendous flood in that island they had been washed down by a mountain torrent, in whose bed they had been long concealed, and worn black. I suppose they had been long buried there, when the island was invaded by General Codrington in 1689, or by Ibbeville in 1715. I may observe that the letters on the Portuguese gold coins denote the settlements where they were coined; as R. for Rio Janeiro, etc., the figures are their value in *Reis*, an imaginary coin of account, so that a five moidore piece, containing 20,000, makes a man very rich, in figures; but really possessing but thirty dollars. The edges were not milled, and much injured by villainy; and when they were milled, they were not clipped and mutilated in so barefaced a manner; and for a time the milling was effectual for their preservation; though at last they suffered. I remember much of the cob-dollar in the weighed-silver, but never in tale. The cob-pistoles I have seen in tale. The gold coins were next regulated, by an arbitrary and illegal measure undoubtedly, but a measure nevertheless absolutely necessary. He issued his proclamation, ordering 2¾d. to be deducted for each grain of gold wanting of the standard weight of each denomination of current

The Jews had the credit of being deeply implicated in the transactions, so dishonorable to us, that led to this beneficial arrangement, as well as being among the first introducers of light and counterfeit money. They have long had a synagogue and are protected in their religious rites; but no legislative enactments have hitherto been permitted, though attempted in their Vestry Bill; rather tolerated than established. They hold real estate, not sugar works, now; for what with their Sabbaths and ours, their holidays and some of ours, they cannot cultivate sugar in so dry and unseasonable an island, with any prospect of success.

They are now confined to one street, Swan Street,[4] its true and very ancient name, and constantly so called by them; but by others Jew Street.

---

gold coins. Immediately they were all weighed, each separate piece wrapped up in paper, with its value written upon it, and its true weight. It was certainly at first very inconvenient, either to receive or pay away considerable sums; and was called " weighed gold." Great honor was observed in these transactions, and very trifling frauds were perpetrated. People seemed tired of cheating. But, being an excellent remittance, the whole very soon disappeared; and an honest, full-weight, milled currency took its place. (For the *Proclamation* vide " Minutes of Council," August 2, 1791, p. 231.)

[4] Swan Street is as old as Cheapside, two of the original streets at the first building of the town. It has not fallen to my lot to find the origin of that name; but I think it very likely to have been so called in honor of Captain Swan, one of the very first setlers here, who, I suppose, from his profession and skill, may have had a hand in laying it out, or resided in it. Ligon speaks of " one Captain Swan, the antientest and most knowing surveyor there." He drew the first map of the island, taken from him by the Governor, Sir Henry Hunckles, and never returned to him. (Vide Ligon, in Loco.) The sinuosity of both streets, I presume, marks the windings of the former beach. Cheapside extended from the new bridge to Shipping Bridge; and in it were the exchange and the butcher's market for meat, but no butchery there.

They are as a people very much reduced, in numbers and wealth; and are little more than retailers. The causes of this declension appear to be chiefly those mentioned below, grow- ing out of the wonderful rise of Liverpool and commerce taking an entire new direction from thence. The canal sys- tem and the machinery in that part of England have raised the commerce of Liverpool beyond any competition, either in prices or expedition; and the Jews having been supplied from London in great measure, they have lost in succession the linen trade, the cotton goods trade, the hardware and pottery trades, and the bullion trade.

By opening the Irish trade, the linen manufactures of Ire- land are now sold here by their own merchants or agents, at the cheapest possible rates; and so very completely, that the very word " Holland," which denoted fine linen, has given place to " Irish "; those linens having been formerly imported into England, from Germany, through Holland. The same fate has befallen the delph wares, which have given place to the more elegant and cheap manufactures of " Etruria " and the potteries. Manchester supplies us most abundantly with her cottons, and almost supersedes the East India cottons; and the hardwares of Birmingham and Sheffield are sold here by their own agents; and so are those from Manchester. The bullion trade is lost by our receiving only perfect and heavy coins; and being supplied abundantly with them by the government, in pay to her garrisons, etc.

APPENDIX A.

Ordered that the consideration (of the Memorial?) of the Jews and Foreigners brought from Brazele to this Island, be presented at the next sitting of ye Governor, Council and Assembly. (" Min- utes of Council," November 8, 1654.)

APPENDIX B.

Whereas it appears to this Board that the Jews in this Island are very prejudicial to Trade, by not buying the Produce of this Island; but, on the contrary, Ship off all the ready money they can get, It is ordered that the Solicitor General[5] and Queen's Counsel procure a list of what Negroes belong to the several Jews in this Island, and that they prepare a Proclamation to Revive, and put in Execution a Law relating to Jews keeping negroes. ("Minutes of Council," July 9, 1705, p. 83.)

II.

MENTION OF THE JEWS IN THE RECORDS OF BARBADOS,
BY J. GRAHAM CRUICKSHANK, ESQ.

(1655)   On the petition of several Jews, it is ordered that, behaving themselves civilly and doing nothing to disturb the peace, they shall enjoy the privileges and laws of the Island relating to foreigners and strangers.   ("Council Minutes," Lucas' copy.)

(1670)   Petition of Jews in St. Michael's Town, that they are unequally taxed by the Vestry.

(1681) · Objection to Jews' testimony in cases where Christians were involved.   They would swear only on the five books of Moses, and not on the Holy Gospel.   Ordered: That their testimony be admitted, ·they swearing as their religion allowed.

(1682)   Raphael de Mercado to appear before Grand Sessions for importing and vending light Spanish money.

(1705)   It appearing to the Council that the Jews are very prejudicial to trade, by not buying the produce of the Island, but, on the contrary, shipping off all the ready money they can get: It is ordered that the Solicitor General and Queen's Counsel procure a list of what negroes belong to the several Jews in the Island and that they prepare a proclamation to revise and put in execution a law relating to Jews' keeping negroes.

NOTE.—Lucas (Vol. 29) mentions an early Act (1688) prohib-

---

[5] N. B. Chilton, the Attorney General, was confined in Gaol by sentence of the Court of Grand Sessions—and suspended at this time.   Rawlin, Solicitor General; William Walker, the Queen's Counsel.

iting Jews and others not employed in agriculture from keeping
more than one negro each. I gather that the Jews made a good
deal of their money by purchasing and hiring out negroes; and
this order by Council was intended, evidently, to place them
under disability in that direction.

(1750)   Case of the kidnapped Portuguese, brought to Barbados and sold to Jews unjustly for a term of years.

NOTE.—There were also some laws all the titles to which, at
least, are given by Rawlins and Hall.

Adding to these notes:—Far, as the Jews were outside my
field—it may be remarked that, from the number of Jews who
lived and traded in it, Swan Street was at one time commonly
known as *Jew Street.*[6] An advertiser in the Barbados *Mercury* for March 16, 1805, says: ". . . . Letters may be left
at Mr. Hunt's, in Jew Street." And Mr. Hawker says that
even forty years ago the street was so known. The stores
there, I was told, had doors leading from one to another, be-
cause, said my informant, the Jews " lived so loving." They
had a peculiar custom of presenting every new Governor with
what was known as " Jew Pie," viz., a crust covering a pile
of gold coins. Omitting this present to one Governor, " ruc-
tions " were the result. I forget how the row was settled.

The Jews in Barbados are now a feeble folk, numbering
scarce half a dozen, headed by the Baezas. I visited the
synagogue which stands at the corner of Synagogue and
Magazine[7] lanes. Behind the wall, in the graveyard, lie about
a thousand tombstones, very close to one another. A favorite
engraving on them is an axman cutting down the unfruitful
tree. A few of the inscriptions are in English, but most in
Hebrew. The oldest tomb I made out was that of David
Raphael Mercado, merchant (perhaps he who imported and
vended the light Spanish money) who died August 14, 1685.
When the late Rev. Daniels was alive, services used to be held

---

[6] After Surveyor Swann, whom Ligon mentions.

[7] From its leading to the powder magazine, which stood about
where the Free Library now stands, then outside the town.

in the synagogue every Saturday morning. But since his death in 1905, and the appointment of no successor services are held only on festivals, by Mr. Joshua Baeza, merchant, in Bridgetown. The synagogue is opened every Saturday morning for anyone who cares to go there to pray, but no one goes. The lamp is always kept burning before the Ark, and I believe ten Mosaical scrolls are *in* the Ark, in good preservation. But the synagogue lacks a congregation.

Within the churchyard walls is another building where the caretaker stays. He tells me that, many years ago, there used to be a school there where Jews in Bridgetown sent their children, daily, to be taught by a rabbi. There was also in the building a room where poor Jews coming to the island were lodged until they found something to do.

The caretaker further said that at Speightstown there used to be a synagogue which was destroyed in the 1831 hurricane, and never rebuilt.

The quiet of the synagogue and surrounding yard, in Bridgetown, is extraordinary in the heart of a busy and congested city.

LAWS OF BARBADOS (HALL'S EDITION).

Among those noted as obsolete, etc.:

33. Private. An Act to make Captain Ham a free denizen, March 3, 1646.

208. Concerning the Denization of certain Jews herein named, July 2, 1662.

WILLS AT SOMERSET HOUSE.

Reference mark Pett 134. Jamaica property—Captain John Moses, of H. M. S. "Anglesea," 23rd Oct. 1703—12th March 1704, Commission to Wm. Moses, Brother.

Reference mark Browning 150. Peter Passataigre of St. Michael's, Barbados, Planter. Will dated 1716, proved 1719.

There is a will of Sampson, of Antigua. This was apparently another Jewish family. Query whether these were Jews?

12

III.

DOMESTIC STATE PAPERS—1655—(I-92).

WARRANTS OF THE PROTECTOR AND COUNCIL.

·1655, April 27th.   For Abr. de Mercadò, M. D., Hebrew, with David Raphael de Mercado, his son, to go to Barbados, where he has an order from His Highness to exercise his profession.

IV.

EXTRACT FROM LETTERS ON SLAVERY, ETC., BY WILLIAM DICKSON, LONDON, 1789.

., (p. 138.)   The Alms House in Bridgetown for the reception of the (white) Poor is the only apology for a Hospital belonging to Barbados.

But, from the *Barbados Mercury* of October 28, 1786, I perceive that a subscription was opened on July 7, for establishing "THE BARBADOES GENERAL DISPENSARY, *for the relief of the Sick poor."* .

Of this charity His Excellency Governor Parry and his lady, with a considerable number of other ladies and gentlemen, liberally contributed; and the active Humanity of that able physician Doctor Handy was particularly useful in promoting it.   Be the effects and the *duration* of this charity what they may, the public spirit and Humanity which actuated the founders of it, do them much honour.

From that honour far be it from me to detract; but, justice to a humble remnant of a once highly·favoured State calls upon me to observe, that, of the sum subscribed to this charity, upwards of one tenth was contributed collectively and individually by the HEBREW NATION; though their numbers fall short of one twentieth of the white inhabitants of Barbadoes, and not one hundredth part of the property of the Island is in their hands.   Sir, this despised (not to say *oppressed*) but peaceable, loyal and, I will add, *venerable,* people, still remember, as they were commanded, the affliction of their forefathers, in the land of Egypt. This surely is an amiable principle; and, for the peculiarity of their other tenets, while they disturb not society, they are not accountable to man. It is remarkable that they were enjoined to "spoil the Egyptians,"—their oppressors—in order, no doubt to vindicate for themselves the wages due for their servitude.

V.

EXTRACT FROM A POEM ENTITLED BARBADOES, BY M. J. CHAPMAN.[8]

See the rare date! whose branches dropt with gold,
And drest with flowers, the sons of Israel hold;
In solemn pomp proceeding, when còmes round
The feast of Tabernacles . . . . .

Note from page 91.

The Jews in this Island, who have given a name to one of the best streets in Bridge-Town, used to carry in processions on the Festival I have mentioned, branches of the Date-tree, gilt and dressed with flowers. It is interesting to observe them adhering to all the rites and ceremonies which can keep alive in their minds the memories of their "pleasant land." They have successfully claimed the respect of their fellow-colonists, and have always been well treated by those whom Mr. Montgomery happily calls "the funguses of the Earth" —the West Indians.[9]

[8] Published in London in 1833, in a volume of verse entitled, "Barbados and other Poems." (page 12.)

[9] Compare articles on the Jews of Barbados in *Publications of the American Jewish Historical Society*, No. 5, pp. 57-61, 90-99 (Dr. H. Friedenwald); No. 1, pp. 105-108 (Dr. Cyrus Adler); No. 2, pp. 95-97 (M. J. Kohler); No. 12, pp. 40-42 (L. Hühner), and the article on "Barbados," by Dr. Herbert Friedenwald, in Vol. III of the *Jewish Encyclopedia*, which utilized E. S. Daniel's "Extract from the Various Records of the Early Settlement of Jews in Barbados," privately printed, 1899. See *supra*, pp. 16, 17.

VI.

DOMESTIC STATE PAPERS—1662-1664—(68-90).

1662-63, February, No. 138. Grants of Denization to James Gayo and Jeronimo Rodriques Resio, living in Barbados, provided they take the Oath of Allegiance before the Chief Magistrate there.

1663, June 22, No. 104. Warrant for a Grant to Toros (Francis?) Lord Willoughby, and Lawrence Hyde of the sole use for 14 years, in Barbados and the other Caribee Islands, of a Sugar Mill newly invented by David de Mercato, with power to employ therein Mercato, or any others whom they may think fit.

1664, January 2. Warrant for a Grant to Francis, Lord Willoughby of Parham, and Lawrence Hyde, second son of the Lord Chancellor, for 21 years, of the sole making and framing of Sugar Mills, after a new manner invented by David de Mercado, who is desirous of the said Grant to be made to them, they giving him all due encouragement.

VII.

THE OLDEST JEWISH TOMBSTONES IN BARBADOS.

(1)   Sᴀ
DOEMCVRTADOARON
DEMERCADO QVE
FAIESEO EM 9
DE ADAR 5420

This is engraved on the stone just as written, without any punctuation. Properly it would be:

Do Em Curtado, Aron De Mercado, Que Faieso Em q de Adar 5420 (1660).

(2) Here Lyeth yᵉ Body of David Raphael De Mercado Merchant who Departed this world yᵉ 14ᵗʰ of August 1685.

Sepultur A do Bemanenturado De Dauid Raphael De Mercado Que Faleceo Sm 24 de Menahem Anᵒ 5445 Sua Alma Goze da Gloria.

A Hebrew inscription on the tomb corresponds with these.

CPSIA information can be obtained
at www.ICGtesting.com
Printed in the USA
LVHW080226040219
606202LV00082B/1397/P